ULTIMATE COMIC ART

DRAWING MYSTICAL HEROES

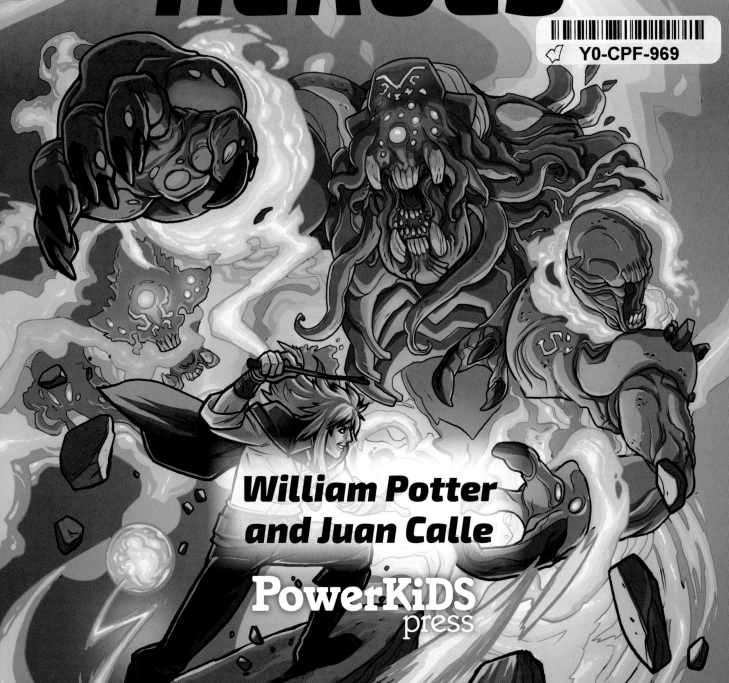

William Potter and Juan Calle

PowerKiDS
press

CONTENTS

CAST A SPELL...

It's a crazy world out there, and it's about to get even wilder. With charms, spells, and supernatural powers, mystic heroes are an exciting part of the superhero team!

LET'S MAKE COMICS

Whether you are bursting with ideas, or have one amazing character to build a story for, we'll help you get your imagination onto the page. Through guides and advice, we'll get you started with drawing techniques and help you create your very own comic strip.

STEPS AHEAD

We're going to start by introducing you to four mystical heroes. Then we'll look at magical realms, clever costumes, drawing spells, and how to put all your mystical adventures onto paper.

Prepare to enter a new realm. You will need to summon all of your magical drawing skills to weave spells, draw powerful RELICS, and bring strange new worlds to life.

BODY MATTERS

When you can draw a figure with accurate proportions, your characters will look more realistic. Superheroes and villains often have exaggerated muscular physiques — some may even have animal or alien features!

The human body is symmetrical, with the bones and muscles on the left matching those on the right.

Men's bodies are often wide at the shoulders and chests, then narrower at the hips. Women's bodies are often narrow at the waist and wider at the hips, like the number 8.

All human bodies are about eight heads tall. The waist is about three heads down from the top of the body, and the hands reach midway down the thigh.

TOP TIP

You don't have to give all of your comic book characters an athletic build. Use different heights and body shapes so that readers find it easier to tell them apart.

When you draw a person standing up straight, you should be able to draw a straight line from the top of their head down through their waist, to their knees, and through the center of their feet. Their shoulders should push out as far as their bottom, while their chest pushes out as far as their toes.

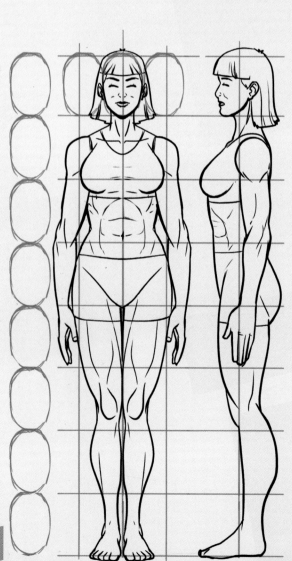

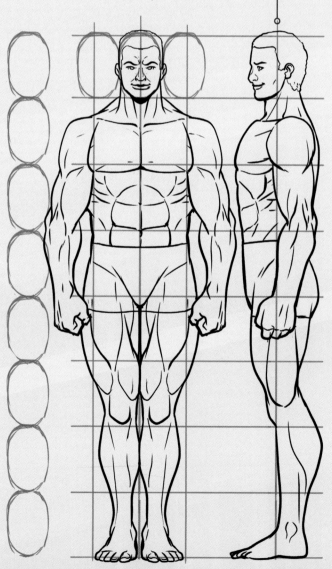

FACE TIME

Faces have their own proportions, with eyes and ears about halfway down the head. Here are average faces you can use for reference.

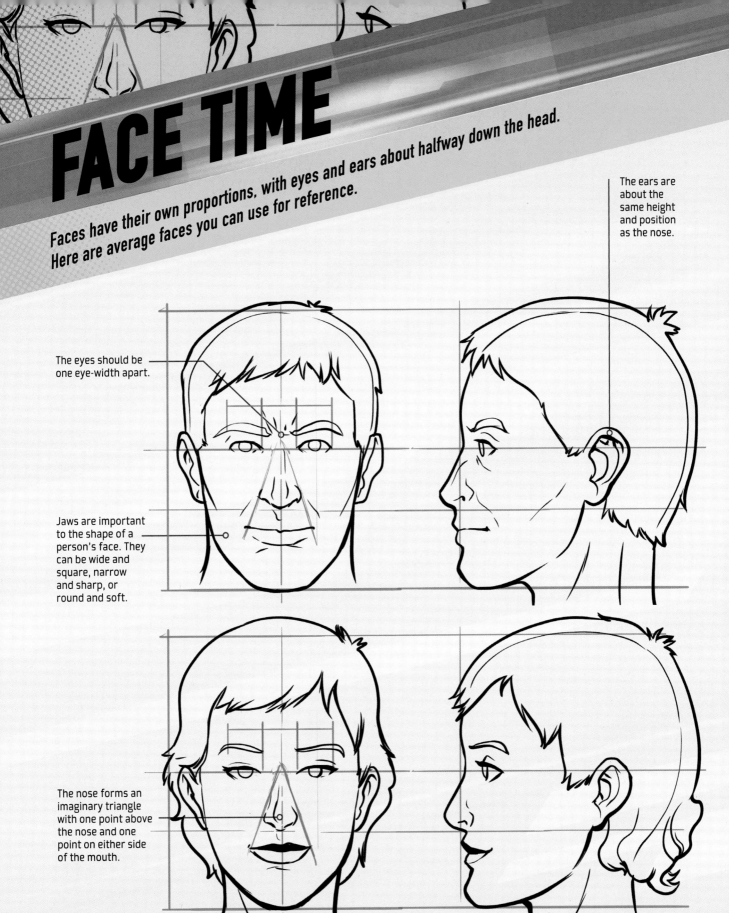

The ears are about the same height and position as the nose.

The eyes should be one eye-width apart.

Jaws are important to the shape of a person's face. They can be wide and square, narrow and sharp, or round and soft.

The nose forms an imaginary triangle with one point above the nose and one point on either side of the mouth.

Look at your friends' and family members' faces. You will see many variations. Sketch the details you see and study their hairstyles. You can use traits like these to make each of your comic characters unique.

FROM START TO FINISH

If you're brimming with ideas, you can jump straight into drawing your comic book. But for most creators, a good page of comic art requires a bit of preparation.

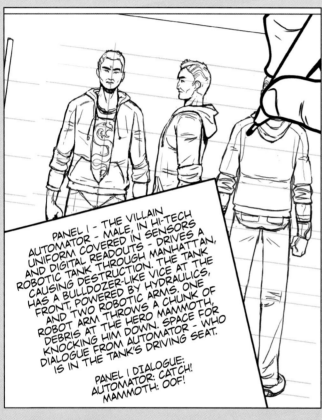

PANEL 1 – THE VILLAIN AUTOMATOR – MALE, IN HI-TECH UNIFORM COVERED IN SENSORS AND DIGITAL READOUTS – DRIVES A ROBOTIC TANK THROUGH MANHATTAN, CAUSING DESTRUCTION. THE TANK HAS A BULLDOZER-LIKE VICE AT THE FRONT, POWERED BY HYDRAULICS, AND TWO ROBOTIC ARMS. ONE ROBOT ARM THROWS A CHUNK OF DEBRIS AT THE HERO MAMMOTH, KNOCKING HIM DOWN. SPACE FOR DIALOGUE FROM AUTOMATOR – WHO IS IN THE TANK'S DRIVING SEAT.

PANEL 1 DIALOGUE:
AUTOMATOR: CATCH!
MAMMOTH: OOF!

1. THE SCRIPT

First, plan your story. Think about the characters who appear in the adventure. What do they look like, what do they wear, and how do they behave? Then, write your story with notes on the action that will take place on each page.

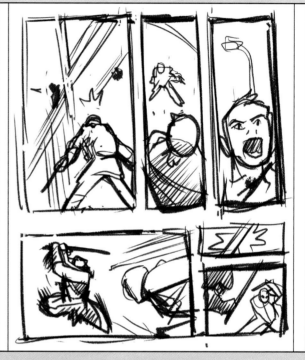

2. THUMBNAILS

Now you can map out a page. These first small, rough sketches for page layouts are called **THUMBNAILS**. When you're happy with the layout, you can move to a larger sheet of paper and prepare for the finished artwork.

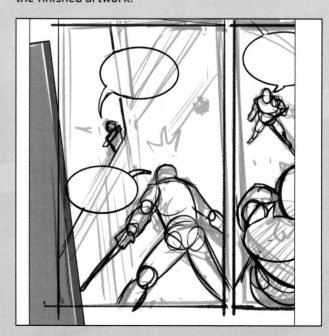

3. THE PANELS

Draw the panels lightly on the page and mark where the **SPEECH BALLOONS** will go. Then you can start drawing details in pencil, starting wherever you like on the page.

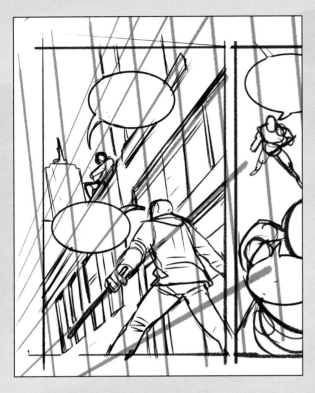

4. PERSPECTIVE

Guidelines for **PERSPECTIVE** help create a 3D environment for many scenes. You can start drawing your characters as stick figures so that you get their poses and positions right.

5. PENCILS

Draw the final details in pencil. Add ruled lines to the speech balloons and write the dialogue between them.

6. COLORING IN

Go over the pencil sketches in ink with a pen or brush, including the panels and speech balloons. Once the ink is dry, you can erase the pencil lines. Finally, it's time for the colors!

SUPERNATURAL SQUAD

Who will come forward to defend Earth from supernatural forces? Here are some suggestions for arcane warriors and masters of magic.

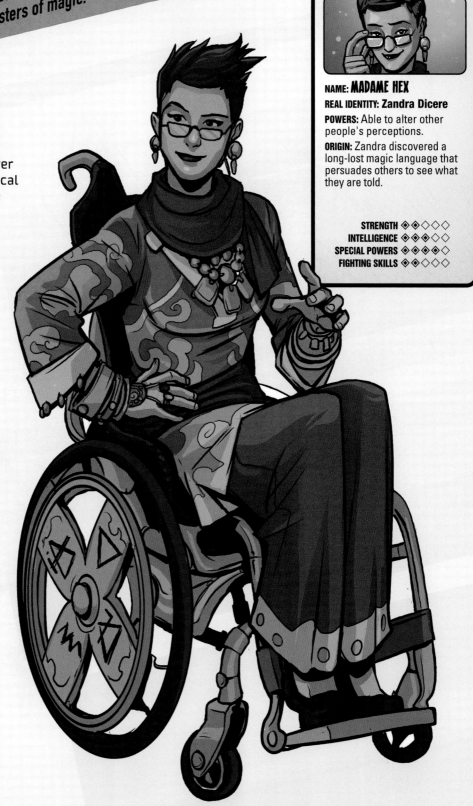

NAME: MADAME HEX

REAL IDENTITY: Zandra Dicere

POWERS: Able to alter other people's perceptions.

ORIGIN: Zandra discovered a long-lost magic language that persuades others to see what they are told.

STRENGTH ◆◆◇◇◇
INTELLIGENCE ◆◆◆◇◇
SPECIAL POWERS ◆◆◆◆◇
FIGHTING SKILLS ◆◆◇◇◇

KNOWLEDGE IS POWER

Where will your mystic character derive their power from? Madame Hex's magical power comes from the use of language to convince others to see what she wants them to. With her powers of persuasion, she weaves words into reality. Persuasion is a strength equal to physical force.

STRENGTH TAKES MANY FORMS

Many of the greatest superheroes are hugely powerful in some ways, but **VULNERABLE** in others. This creates an interesting contrast. Madame Hex has needed a wheelchair to aid her mobility since she was a child, but that didn't stop her from becoming a vital and powerful member of Earth's magic defense force.

CUTTING A DASH

Magical heroes rarely wear the tight spandex costumes popular with muscular superheroes. Ethan Ether thinks of himself as one in a long line of magicians, so he wears a short cloak like a nineteenth-century man of magic, but with a modern swagger. Magic is the new rock 'n' roll, you know!

GROWING UP

Ethan's father, Edward, was also a magician, but Ethan is very different from his dad. Edward was thoughtful and restrained, but Ethan is flamboyant and loves to show off his magical talents. This vanity could be his downfall. If your characters have flaws, part of your story can be showing how they learn from their mistakes to become better heroes.

NAME: ETHAN ETHER

REAL IDENTITY: Ethan Etherington

POWERS: Able to channel the powers of past magicians with the same wand passed through generations.

ORIGIN: At age 16, Ethan received the gift of a wand from his missing magician father, whose spirit guides him.

STRENGTH ◇◇◇◇◇
INTELLIGENCE ◇◇◇◇◇
SPECIAL POWERS ◇◇◇◇◇
FIGHTING SKILLS ◇◇◇◇◇

DO YOUR HOMEWORK

Ezora is from Louisiana and has a Creole background. Creole people have their own culture and language, so Ezora might sometimes use a few Creole words and may refer to her home when talking to her teammates. If you create a character with a background different from your own, it is essential to do research to get the details right. What you find out could inspire a new story!

DRAWING THE INVISIBLE

Dream Diviner's pose shows her reaching out and concentrating as she communicates with a spirit. She can see and hear beings that are dead or alive in nearby dimensions. These beings are invisible to everyone else. Of course, in a comic book, you can draw the ghosts and beings she sees, but make it clear that no one else can see them.

NAME: DREAM DIVINER

REAL IDENTITY: Ezora Aurieux

POWERS: Can communicate with the spirit realm and see other-dimensional beings.

ORIGIN: Born during a unique alignment of astral events, Aurieux has the gift of "spirit sight" which lets her see beyond the material realm.

STRENGTH ◈◈◈◈◇
INTELLIGENCE ◈◈◇◇◇
SPECIAL POWERS ◈◈◈◈◈
FIGHTING SKILLS ◈◈◇◇◇

MAGICAL TRANSFORMATION

With the right enchantments, even a down-to-earth guy can be turned into a mystic warrior. As a soldier, Ángel Vasquez was used to fighting traditional wars, but then a mystic cult put him through a powerful ritual. Now he is protected from supernatural attacks, and his soul-fire sword can harm the otherworldly monsters he faces.

NAME: QUESTER

REAL IDENTITY: Ángel Vasquez

POWERS: Combat skills, pain-resistant. Sword fires power blasts and raises force field.

ORIGIN: Soldier Vasquez was captured by occultists who put him through a ritual that turned him into a supernatural warrior.

STRENGTH	◆◆◆◇◇
INTELLIGENCE	◆◆◇◇◇
SPECIAL POWERS	◆◆◆◇◇
FIGHTING SKILLS	◆◆◆◇◇

MODERN MEDIEVAL

Historic warriors are a great source for character and costume inspiration. Quester is a modern-day warrior in a medieval-style armor, replacing heavy metal with tough, lightweight materials, such as Kevlar. He's not afraid of using tech on supernatural enemies, either—his sword fires power blasts and can raise a force field.

MODERN MAGICIAN

Through the use of mystic artifacts, Charm can summon benevolent spirits to help her wage war against evil. Follow the steps to summon her to life, too.

1. WIRE FRAME

Start drawing Charm's pose using a stick figure with an oval for the head and circles for joints. Give her a dramatic **POSTURE**, but make sure the proportions are correct for her body, arms, and legs.

2. BLOCK FIGURE

Now fill out Charm's figure using 3D shapes. Even though she will be wearing a flowing dress, you need to figure out where her legs fit beneath the gown.

NAME: CHARM

REAL IDENTITY: Charmaine Bryant

POWERS: Can summon supernatural creatures to her aid through the use of mystical artifacts.

ORIGIN: After trying to save a homeless woman from mystical attack, Charmaine received her magical jewels as a reward.

STRENGTH	◈◈◇◇◇
INTELLIGENCE	◈◈◈◈◇
SPECIAL POWERS	◈◈◈◈◇
FIGHTING SKILLS	◈◈◈◈◇

3. FINISHED PENCILS

When you are happy with the figure, you can draw the basic shape of her dress flowing over her body. Her clothing follows her curves, with wind from the right blowing her skirt to the left. A scarf curls around her neck, and her long hair flows wildly in the wind.

4. INKS

Carefully ink the figure, adding long folds in her skirt and mystic patterns on her jacket. The outline of the spirit which Charm is conjuring can now be seen, following the position of her arms.

The spirit coming from Charm's amulet is partway on its journey from another dimension. Only the top half of its body is visible, but you can still build up its form using a wire frame and 3D shapes. Since it is not completely solid, use colored instead of black outlines for the finished artwork, and show parts of the background through its body.

5. COLORS

The finished colors add highlights and shadows to Charm's hair and dress, as well as the ghostly spirit. The pale blue lights shining from Charm's eyes show that she is using her supernatural powers.

MYSTIC REALM

In the magical Dread Dimension, the rules of perspective don't apply. Here's how to ground your mystical heroes in a realm without reason.

1. THE ROUTE

In this scene, Quester the supernatural warrior has to find his way across a magical landscape to reach the Kingdom of Curses. The hero needs something to stand on and a path to the kingdom's ruins. The path has many curves.

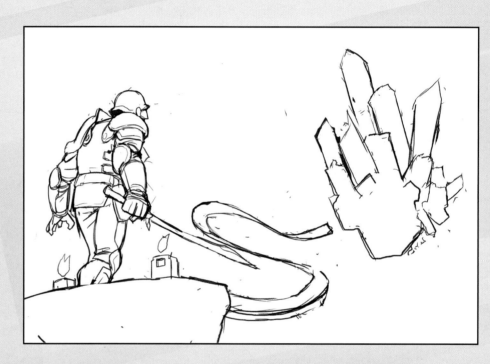

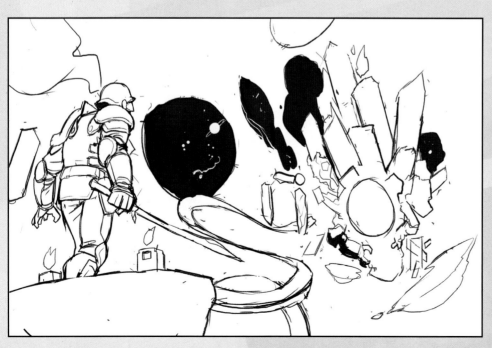

2. STRUCTURE

Before you add any details, mark out the large shapes, such as clouds, floating islands, and areas of darkness, to give the weird landscape some structure and to help lead your eye toward the hero's destination.

3. WILD WORLD

It's time to let your imagination flow! Break up the path with steps and strange doorways, and then add abstract shapes and monstrous creatures to the weird realm.

4. THE PATH IS REVEALED

The finished, inked scene looks bizarre, but you can still find your way around it. The reader may not know what every magical thing is, but the objects look solid, and there are enough familiar shapes to lead both the reader and Quester in the right direction.

WIZARD'S WARDROBE

This wizard may be from the present day, but you'll still need some traditional art skills to make his clothing fold and flow in a realistic fashion.

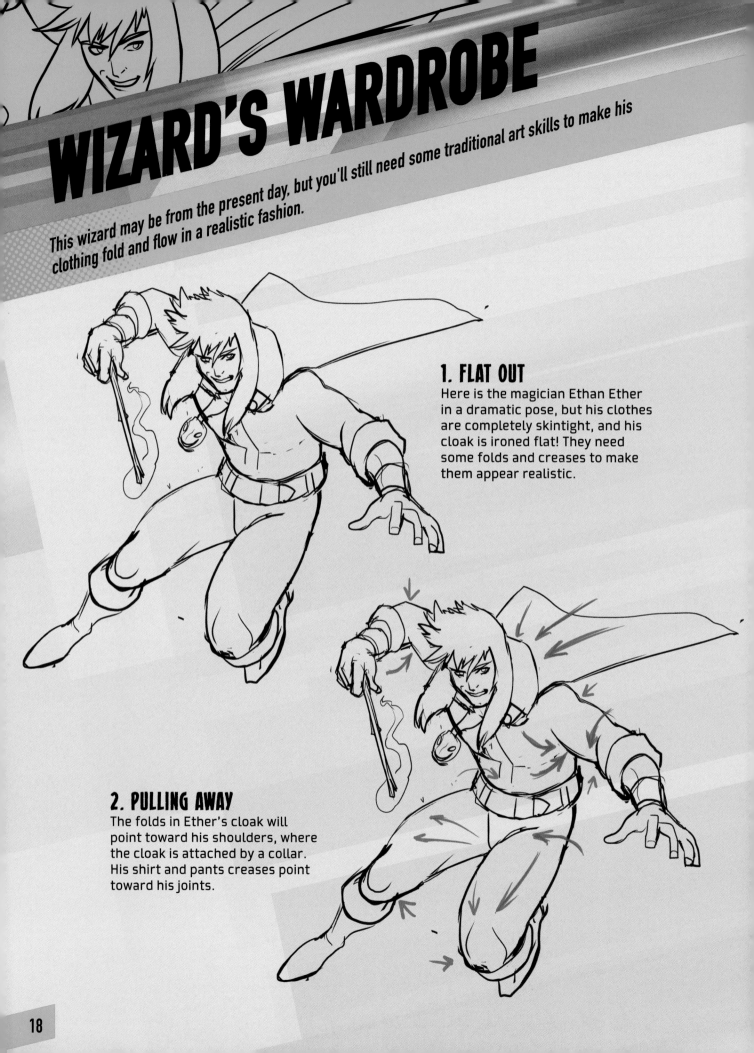

1. FLAT OUT

Here is the magician Ethan Ether in a dramatic pose, but his clothes are completely skintight, and his cloak is ironed flat! They need some folds and creases to make them appear realistic.

2. PULLING AWAY

The folds in Ether's cloak will point toward his shoulders, where the cloak is attached by a collar. His shirt and pants creases point toward his joints.

FOLD OUT

Increase your crease knowledge with this example of how a pair of pants folds over the body. See how the long folds point toward the knees, where the material is stretched tight. Creases appear behind the knees where the material is baggier.

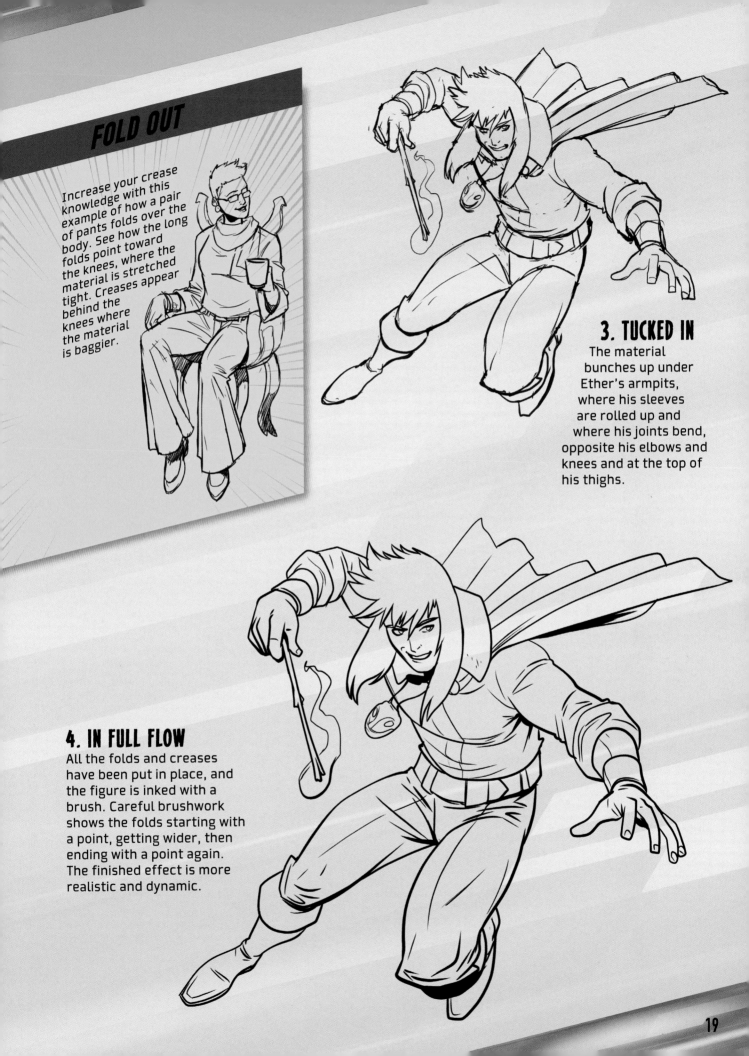

3. TUCKED IN

The material bunches up under Ether's armpits, where his sleeves are rolled up and where his joints bend, opposite his elbows and knees and at the top of his thighs.

4. IN FULL FLOW

All the folds and creases have been put in place, and the figure is inked with a brush. Careful brushwork shows the folds starting with a point, getting wider, then ending with a point again. The finished effect is more realistic and dynamic.

MAGIC TRICKS

What does a spell look like? You can easily show the effect, but you'll also need to show the spell-casting.

SPELL

◄ Here, Charm is twisting her fingers into special spell positions. Circles of magic light surround her hand, and streams of mystic force radiate outward, ready to be directed at their target.

FORCE SHIELD

➤ In this case, the magical object—a protective shield—is drawn in midair. A light trail shows its boundary, while a semitransparent color shows where the shield is in place.

TOP TIP

While superhero power bolts are usually shown taking a direct path, mystical spells often follow curving routes as if they have their own minds—perhaps they do!

RUNES

◄ Spells may be in an ancient language. The magic "words" in runes and symbols appear to float in the air, as they demonstrate their power.

BOLTS

➤ Charm has generated bolts of mystic energy to strike a foe. Once summoned into the palms of her hand, she hurls them toward her enemy.

21

RELICS OF POWER

Objects hold great power for magicians. Here are some relics worth collecting for your mystic heroes. Every magical object should have its own story... what will yours be?

AMULET

➤ This amulet holds the Orb of Voltain, a stone of ancient, possibly extradimensional origin. The sparkles in the gem suggest a whole galaxy is contained within it. Worn around a magician's neck, it offers protection against evil incantations.

BOOK

➤ Containing the wisdom of the witch Magluthra, this book of spells and remedies was kept safe by the Order of Z'Tor for centuries until the evil Lord Tralon stole it from their library. The worn bindings and leather show its age. A strong lock suggests its secrets need protecting.

STAFF

➤ Cut from the same willow as the cane of the legendary magician Merlin, this staff of power is inscribed with powerful spells. It can lead its bearer away from danger and discharge the lightning of wrath upon enemies. Look at old languages, such as Viking runes, then design your own language for writing spells.

CRYSTAL

◄ Stolen from the Cave of the Fair Elves, this crystal contains a source of fairy magic. Combined with the right words, it allows its bearer to use many powerful enchantments. Mystical relics often change hands and can lead to a story with good and evil magicians fighting for ownership.

FORCE SWORD

➤ The Nornsword, wrought from rare norn metal, can cut and wound supernatural beings immune to other earthly weapons. Anointed with a spell of revelation by the wizard Amouthrir, it glows when faced with untruths. Adding a history, unique source, or engraving to a familiar weapon can turn it into an object of magic.

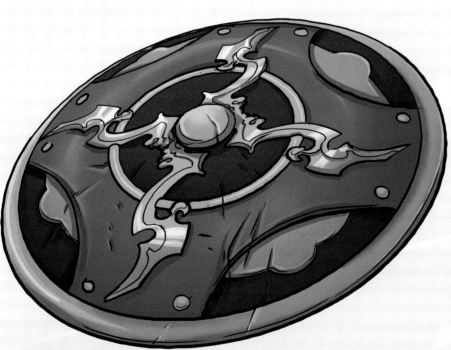

SHIELD

▲ The Shield of Styrig is said to be the same one that the wizard-slayer Styrig used to defeat the Coven of Kruel in the world before time. It can deflect any spell, reflecting it back to the one who cast it. Your comic book stories don't have to be set in the present day. Why not invent a magical past that was never described in the history books?

SUPERNATURAL STRIKE

Let's create a dramatic scene full of spells flying in all directions. Earth's champions of the light will need all their magical knowledge to keep the Sastorfrax twins from corrupting our world with darkness.

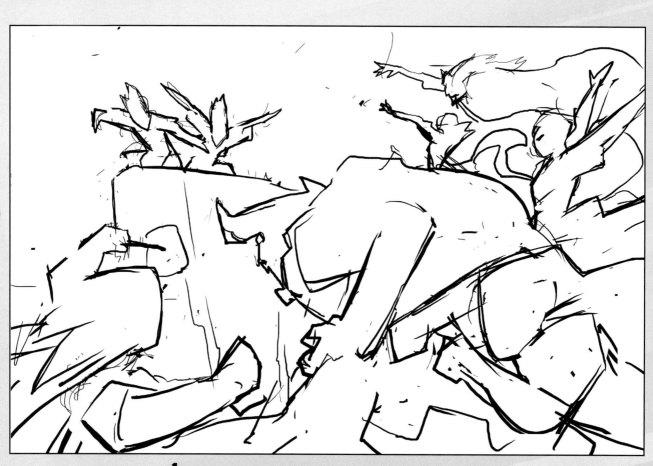

1. Figure out the positions of your heroes and villains in a small thumbnail sketch. The twins stand on a ledge above the heroes, making them appear even more **DOMINANT**.

one of the most powerful dark magic teams.

ORIGIN: The twin children of former Dark Lord Sastorfrax now combine their inherited mystic powers.

NAME: THE SASTORFRAX TWINS

IDENTITY: Guyal and Synge Sastorfrax

POWERS: In unison, they form

STRENGTH	◆◆◆◆◇
INTELLIGENCE	◆◆◆◇◇
SPECIAL POWERS	◆◆◆◆◇
FIGHTING SKILLS	◆◇◇◇◇

2. For the rough pencil sketches, the angle of the villains' ledge has been tilted for a more imposing view. Blue perspective lines show the direction of the action, with the heroes pushing forward to the base of the ledge.

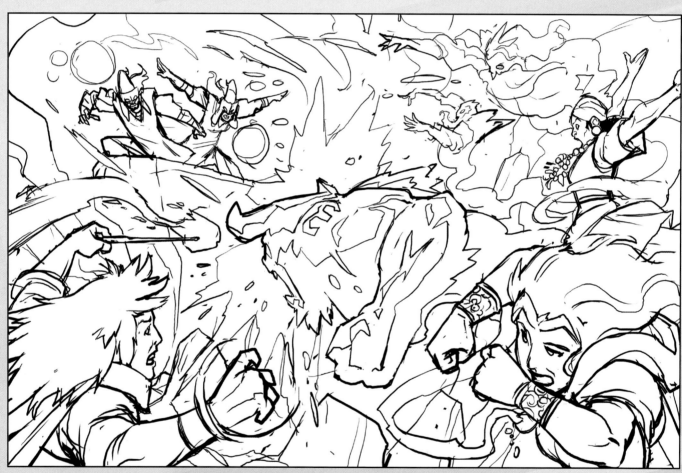

3. Tighten the pencil sketches, and outline a swirling magic storm raging around the twins, while mystic bolts go back and forth between the forces of dark and light.

TOP TIP
Magic spells can take any shape or path. Use them to guide your reader around the action. In this scene, magic swirls lead your eye from the heroes to the villains and back.

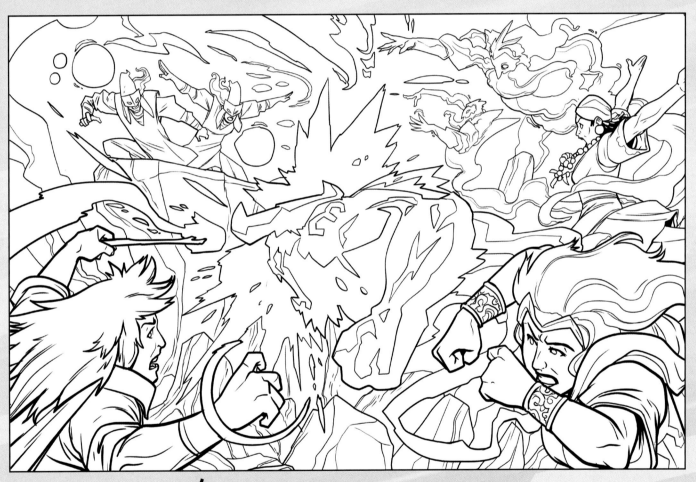

4. Carefully ink the pencil lines you want to keep with a brush or pen. Use a thicker outline for the characters in the foreground—Ether and Charm. You may want to use a color to outline the flashes of magical lightning and the ghostlike beings that Dream Diviner has summoned.

WIZARD WAR

In the finished picture, the whole scene is lit up with bolts of magic power and the eruptions of hot gas from the savage landscape. The outcome of the battle is far from certain.

COVER UP

A front cover needs to grab the attention of a potential reader and give a clue to the excitement inside. Here are the essentials for selling your comic book classic.

You don't always need words on the cover, but in this case, Quester's quote adds to the drama.

Your comic will need a title. Usually, this will be the name of the lead character or team. Take time designing an eye-catching logo.

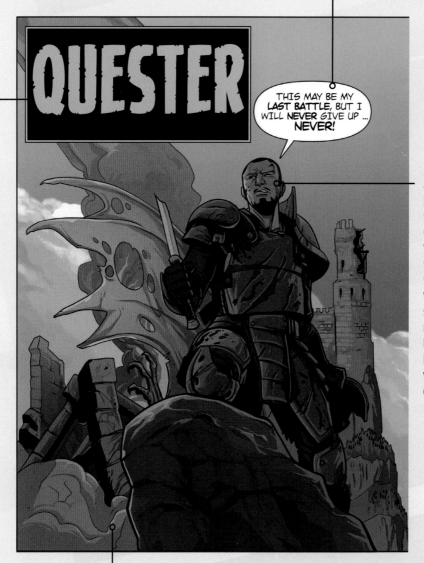

An amazing portrait of your story's hero or a dramatic scene with the hero struggling to survive works well. The image should make readers want to know more—who is this hero? How will he escape certain doom?

The inked outline is bolder than the lines used for the comic story inside, as if it is a blown-up comic panel.

GLOSSARY

ARTIFACT A historical human-made object.

DOMINANT Having power or influence over another.

PERSPECTIVE A way of representing three-dimensional (3D) objects in a picture.

POSTURE The way a figure holds their body when sitting or standing.

RELIC An object of historical interest.

SPEECH BALLOON A shape used in comic panels to hold character dialogue.

THUMBNAIL A rough, small-scale sketch used for planning a page layout.

VULNERABLE Someone who is at risk of physical or emotional harm.

FURTHER INFORMATION

Book to read

Create Your Own Superhero Stories by Paul Moran (Buster Books, 2010)

DC Comics Coloring Book by DC Comics Warner Bros. (Studio Press, 2016)

Drawing Manga: Step by Step by Ben Krefta (Arcturus Publishing, 2013)

Drawing Wizards, Witches and Warlocks by Chris Hart (Sixth and Spring Books, 2009)

How to Draw Wizards, Witches, Orcs and Elves by Steve Beaumont (Arcturus Publishing, 2006)

Stan Lee's How to Draw Superheroes by Stan Lee (Watson-Guptill, 2013)

Write and Draw Your Own Comics by Louise Stowell and Jess Bradley (Usborne, 2014)

Websites

PowerKids Press has developed an online list of websites related to the subject of this book. This site is updated regularly. Please use this link to access the list: **www.powerkidslinks.com/uca/mystical**

INDEX

Published in 2018 by **The Rosen Publishing Group, Inc.**
29 East 21st Street, New York, NY 10010

CATALOGING-IN-PUBLICATION DATA

Names: Potter, William.
Title: Drawing mystical heroes / William Potter and Juan Calle.
Description: New York : PowerKids Press, 2018. | Series: Ultimate comic art | Includes index.
Identifiers: ISBN 9781508154747 (pbk.) | ISBN 9781508154686 (library bound) | ISBN 9781508154563 (6 pack)
Subjects: LCSH: Heroes in art--Juvenile literature. | Fantasy in art--Juvenile literature. | Figure drawing--
    Technique--Juvenile literature. | Comic books, strips, etc.--Technique--Juvenile literature.
Classification: LCC NC1764.8.F37 P68 2018 | DDC 741.5'1--dc23

Text: William Potter
Illustrations: Juan Calle and Info Liberum
Design: Neal Cobourne
Design series edition: Emma Randall
Editor: Joe Harris

Manufactured in the United States of America

CPSIA Compliance Information: Batch BS17PK: For Further Information contact Rosen Publishing, New York, New York at 1-800-237-9932.